we are not wearing helmets

we are not wearing helmets

POEMS

CHERYL BOYCE-TAYLOR

TriQuarterly Books / Northwestern University Press
Evanston, Illinois

TriQuarterly Books
Northwestern University Press
www.nupress.northwestern.edu

Printed in the United States of America

10 9 8 7 6 5 4 3 2 1

Library of Congress Cataloging-in-Publication Data

Names: Boyce-Taylor, Cheryl, 1950– author.
Title: We are not wearing helmets : poems / Cheryl Boyce-Taylor.
Description: Evanston, Illinois : TriQuarterly Books/Northwestern University Press, 2022.
Identifiers: LCCN 2021037400 | ISBN 9780810144231 (paperback) | ISBN 9780810144248 (ebook)
Subjects: LCGFT: Poetry.
Classification: LCC PS3602.O9275 W4 2022 | DDC 811/.6—dc23
LC record available at https://lccn.loc.gov/2021037400

For Deisha Head Taylor,
a daughter, a woman who lifted me.

And for
Rodlyn H. Douglas

The whole country devastated,
only mountains and rivers remain.

—Basho

CONTENTS

ACKNOWLEDGMENTS

I am grateful to the editors of the following publications, where these poems first appeared:

Adrienne: "Adrienne," "Leo"

Black Lesbians: We Are the Revolution: "Beloved Country," "Call Her Delphinium," "Cry," "Turkey Basting"

The Feminist Wire: "A Woman Speaks"

Killens Review of Arts & Letters: "Howl for Maya Angelou" "Pigeon Point, Tobago"

Mom Egg Review: "Ntozake's Crimson Orchids"

Mouths of Rain: "How to Make Art"

Poetry magazine and poets.org (Academy of American Poets): "Devouring the Light"

Small Axe Press: "Glory," "I Am Nothing Compared To"

Soul Sister Review: "Huevos Rancheros & Frozen Margaritas"

Heartfelt gratitude to Ms. Parneshia Jones and the entire TriQuarterly Books/ Northwestern University family.

To the women of Elma's Heart Circle, and to the following individuals who give me constant support and encouragement: Elvis Alves, Sherwin Banfield, Ambriel Floyd Bostic, Malik Izaak Boyce-Taylor, Christian Campbell, Breena Clarke, Steven Fullwood, Aracelis Girmay, Alexis Pauline Gumbs, Ellen Hagan, Sabrina Hayeem-Ladani, JP Howard, Bonnie Rose Marcus, Dennis Nurkse, Dominique Sindayiganza, Mariahadessa Ekere Tallie, Deisha Head Taylor, Samantha Thornhill, Vincent Toro, Donna Lee Weber, and always to my beloved, Desciana Swinger.

I

WE ARE NOT WEARING HELMETS

DEVOURING THE LIGHT, 1968
after Martin Luther King Jr.

The day they killed Martin
we could not return to New York City
our visiting senior class stuck in Huntsville
streets blazed with suffering in that small
Alabama town
in the dull shroud of mourning
the whole world went crazy
devouring whatever light
came through our half-cracked windows.

FIRST AMENDMENT RIGHTS
for Aunt V. on her ninety-ninth birthday

We women stood strong in our madness
in the face of wooden bats   billy clubs
hoses guns mad dogs
in the face of a world that was not ours
a world of dirty twisted money and flies
toss the worms from trees
burn curtains in windows
let the bodies spark
throats scissored open   1967
late into that summer we marched for women's rights
we marched for mothers
we were women married to our rage
against the mad acrobats trying to displace us trying to eject us but this
this was our house
our bodies
our children
our home
we marched long into our aging
gray hair shining
we marched our feet covered in blood
hangers tore us open still we marched   1968
questions of her body
we lit our world on fire
had our illegitimate babies
no father named on the birth certificate
we collected food stamps and project cheese
built cradles tables chairs
heads thrown back we were defiant in our righteousness
our bodies steamed earth
rage became our first self
we marched arm in arm

next day the white woman still refused to say mornin' at the bus
stop!

4

LANDAY FOR FANNIE LOU HAMER

Fannie Lou beat with billy club no /
club dog hose whip chain could cease her fight / not Miss Fannie.

WE ARE NOT WEARING HELMETS

Miss Fannie your voice will weave my words into Congo drums
if I painted my face it would not be the color of surrender
cobalt blue like God's great sky before a rainstorm

not much in this country reminds me of myself
the billy clubs are coming Fannie
already the bombs have begun to fall

will the oppressors place those dull coils of smoke
around their necks
or sell it back to us as precious jewels

I have no more rage poems
was it something my father did
or was it Eve

we have become things to toss
plastic grocery bags the Sunday *Times*
old rusted beach chairs
cigarette butts

we are not wearing helmets or protective suits
the dead are coming Garvey
killers and liars too

outside hyacinths are shrieking
not loud enough to drown the screams

three a.m. moon
a voyeur through sheer blue
curtains of our bedroom window

the lush brown village of her
body creased around mine.

LESSONS: #45

I knew I disliked that man
with his bruise of a mouth
and his dick in flames

most afternoons now I sit at an outdoor café in Bk
coffee in hand and wait for words
like drumbeats to pound
& fall off de side ah meh face

I cannot say what color tiles are in our bathroom
but I can say how many pencils I bought this week
to catch each call to grow a seed   a revolution

every day I am unlearning America
her sticky fingers deep in the hull of brown faded bones

I am still thinking about the cool clay of my first lover's hips
her fingers long impressions of sweeping light
my laughing body rising

she was the reason I tied my head in white and lit red Chango candles
poems falling like Florida water in each corner of the room

to bed we brought our trumpets of girlhood
& sharply oiled faces
her father's hands
my mother's laugh
her dime store pearls

every day I am relearning this America
White Castle gone, summer hydrant & children's laughter
two-story homes replaced with twelve-story high-rise & families dressed like
penguins who look away when you smile & never pay their taxes

HARVEST

1

I cannot write poems
about another Black man beaten

shot, killed, choked to death no,
not another Black man   or woman

I will not visit the damp of death
when the warmth of home leaves a body

I cannot hear again the wounds of Billie's song
it mocks my heart, *don't explain*

I may as well be a pillar of salt
with my mouth sewn shut

gift us dear lord a season of live births
so that we may praise the harvest of our womb

I will listen again to Marvin Gaye
I must relearn *what's going on, there's too many of us dying*

it is my own son's death I fear every day
every day I carry a dark river in my hands

2

when we were kids
my brother and I got piano lessons on credit

we brought sweet governor's plums to Miss Maureen
our piano teacher

we ate ripe mangoes direct from the tree
we were never hungry

I wanted to learn my lessons well
wanted to please my mother

3

wanted to be a maker of random prayers
bless the earth with songs

yuh eh ask meh nah chile
but I tellin yuh anyway

something done come and gone wrong

I would trade mother-of-pearl give you poems ripped naked
from earth's bruised limbs

no more Black lives—

I'm terrified of this scorching
this scent of burning hair

my evening dress holds the scent of blood
I will not will not

carry this sound of wailing in my head
I've come so close to beautiful

but not enough to save our sons
our daughters.

NO MORE WAR POEMS
for David Armstrong

I came home to find my door unlocked
not much in this country reminds me of myself
no bodegas mangoes affordable apartments

no tamarind Jarritos in Bed-Stuy
only Starbucks   Whole Foods   fancy wine stores
nannies   white girls with pit bulls and kombucha

America usta be my dream camp
my golden shoes

I wonder how we will carve this
what sharp knife shall I leave my grandson
somebody please touch this bright bone of longing

was there something important we gave up last year
there are no more war poems
we are not wearing helmets or protective suits

if I die this year love
only love will have her way

PIGEON POINT, TOBAGO

the lifted arms of market lady shine
with the pink and silver glow of fish scales
men with matted locks smile
through half-eaten cigars
teeth the color of black coffee

smells of crab and dumplings
sneak into the cracks of our louvered doors
noon and tourist hide under coconut trees
waiting for sun to shift
their half-lives weighted with rum punch and sunblock

the high-pitch voice of market lady calls
fresh fish fifteen dollars ah pound
fish fresh fifteen—
five dollars   that's it   shouts
a vacationer from beneath a shady tree
twelve   she counters

six   and you clean and cook it   he yells
no man
lord have mercy
mister I have chiren to feed yuh kno   I have chiren

six dollars and not a penny more, he fumes

okay   a'right
six dollars fer de pound
and I clean and cook it

CROSSING RIVERS

There was always
somebody dancing in the rain
burning patchouli
lifting a veil
throwing open dey legs
wailing
birthing
picking names
rocks out of pigeon peas
somebody always
going to the store
looking for a freebie
buying more beer
cigarettes
coffee
frying fish
sifting rice
yelling
cussing
calling us nigga
and bastard
and blackie
asking for blue bills
blowing white rum
spitting Florida water in corners
leaving bread & red candles
behind doors for Chango
dancing in the rain
wailing
birthing

CRY
for Surya

I cannot tell you when the earth shifted
or when the center of its shell broke
poisoning our water
I cannot tell you when the fruit spoiled
leaving bitter dust in our mouths
I cannot tell you how our foremothers survived
or why we are still here

once my grandmother told me
Cheryl, when the baby hiccups
put a black thread on his forehead

I tried that it didn't work
the baby cried and cried
I held him close to my body
until his sound echoed volcanoes
water trees rocks and aching mast of ships

his cries breaking off small bits of skin and bone
as they journeyed through the Middle Passage
his cries the sound of harmattan
of salt of sea

HUEVOS RANCHEROS AND FROZEN MARGARITAS

At Taqueria Tepango I scrape
the last of my refried beans with my fingers
spicy red sauce stinging the corner of my lips
out in the seventy-degree sunshine
first day of spring
I walk slowly along overpriced Myrtle Avenue
now a Hasidic community
a bucket of water unexpectedly thrown from the fifth floor
I look up to see a red-faced boy peeking and grinning
I order his ass outside!

LOTTERY: BROOKLYN

Because their ass is fake as shit
there are three keys for the front door
a camera
a doorman
a book to sign you in
a book to sign you out
there is one padded elevator for deliveries and baby carriages
another for the apartment cleaners
another for the well-dressed unemployed millennial
Gen Z is not allowed on the rooftop garden
unless accompanied by a parent
deliveries can only happen by appointment
in blocks of four-hour intervals
companies must show a COI (certificate of insurance)
if delivering furniture or heavy objects
tenants are mandated to obtain personal insurance
in a cordial conversation with the saleswoman at Crate & Barrel
I ask about my delivery
she ask me if I won a lottery
to get in that building I mean
I flip cock my head and go off on her ass
to prove that I too can be fake as shit
never trust a sweet-faced Caribbean
they got more faces than jobs.

RED WHITE BLUE
Quarantine 2020

Mostly I worry that I will never dance again
carefree with my hips swinging wild
when she returns from shopping I'm scared to cuddle my lover's face

these days small pieces of home torn from limbs
this cold scary country has worn me down   don't
don't go outside without mask and gloves
don't let the doctor touch you
you gonna be sorry if you let them tinker with your organs right now

I felt myself falling under the weight of Covid
news lies and fear
there must be a God whatever we believe

we are walking five to six feet from each other
looking suspiciously at the one pushing the baby carriage behind us

I don't want to sleep with war nipping at my dreams
to feel a piece of rich dark earth falling through my fingers

to sing   hug my grandson
I wish to be brave
wish to be truthful
I wish to leave this country now

I always knew the great America was overrated
Trump's red white blue
a generous lie rigged to my living room window.

II

CRACK ON OUR
FRONT DOOR

WHEN SKY FELL

Always my grandmother's belt
her rage swift and painful

she'd throw a rock or shoe or book
if she called and you didn't answer

my mother's glitter arms
her fish body slicing water

once I fell asleep on her back
in a river that glowed and grew sweet lemons

her orchid wreath of wet locks
glowing when the sky fell

and if I say *father*
how can I unload that

father son wishbone
ghost or back of my knee

drunk willful womanizing
what we lost that year

after begging for months
your father offers six dollars
for your week at summer camp

I was happy
had been for a long time

until he said
tell your mother I'm no money tree

his fist a small prickly pomerac in my throat
a husky chimney hanging from his mouth

here is your father
selling all your secrets

here is your father
facing you down like a woman

ten and staring down shame
could not look at cousin Avi standing next to me

then the crude boat of my lips opened
tripping the skeletal frame of my teeth

and me neck thrown back
hollering from my big Oshun mouth
fuck you into the red traffic of my island

HUFFY

Cousin Villma had the first Huffy bike I ever saw
a fat green ugly thing more grasshopper than breadfruit leaf
more lime-green than watercress
its tires plump as cousin Villma's thighs and although RayRay,
    Teetee, and I spent all
morning dusting washing and folding
doing Villma's chores we never got our promised ride
then one night RayRay threw a worm in Villma's hair
she tumbled over the handrails her braid caught
in the open weave of the yellow carrier basket
she landed in the jump-up-and-kiss-me bush
knees skinned and bleeding
we left her lying there cussing and moaning
while we took turns flying down the hill
over the soft grass tufts on our way to heaven.

CALL ME MONKEY

The year I was twelve Mom registered me in a new school
In my class that year were three other Cheryls
Mom registered me as Allison
I loved that name
it was the third of three names she christened me with
she dared Ammy and Jackie my two best friends to call me
      anything but Allison

once in New York City my aunt called me Cherry
my classmates called me coconut
and monkey because of my Caribbean accent
even the teacher snickered when I spoke
it hurt

on my first spelling test I got 100
most of my classmates got under 70
I was the only one laughing then
at recess I made three new friends

it was the day for vanilla egg creams
and snickering at fat Don when he offered
a walk to the store

JUNE PLUMS

My father is forever my child
when I arrive in Trinidad he begs for bread and wine
he begs for new crisp American dollars
and a white shirt for his sister's funeral
at sixteen he begs me to ask my mother to take him back
even though he loves another woman
he loves my mother more   he says
my father shows me a picture of a small freckle-faced child
swears me to secrecy
promise that I will not tell my mother about the boy child he's hiding
he takes me to the ocean to meet my little brother
August sea still warm
I make a necklace of
seaweeds for his gleaming neck
my father thanks me for the boy's gift
throws himself into my arms
rage eating me like June plums.

wonder if he loves this light-skin boy more than me?

LEO

I should have photographed the crack on the front door of my first home
how the afternoon light leaned in
I'd stand there taking in the warmth
watching the boys play soccer in the crisp dirt
watching Leo try to keep up with his one short leg

for a long time I wished my son would have a baby
I even wished I had another baby with my new wife
it would be a boy   we would call him Leo

I buried my son's first tooth near the wilting stalks
of the arsenic-blue salvia bush
so much ritual went into the penance of burying that first tooth

small pail of water
an old green plastic shovel
two seashells one broken
the other perfect in shades of pale carmine pink
a piece of striped peppermint candy
and a sliver of paper with the name Leo in slanted script
I called the tooth Leo

Leo was the caramel-brown boy who hit me
and ran away expecting me to run after him
he returned the next day with peppermints and an orange for me

everyone called him sugar
I called him Leo

two weeks into the school year Leo disappeared from the first grade
gossip had it that his father killed his mother and returned to Venezuela
others said his mother killed his father and ran away with Leo

whatever the story I always wanted to do a special ritual in his name.

ROAD TO BANJUL

In Banjul the girl with the dirty scarf tied around her head
gives me a mango

I give her Neruda's *Twenty Love Poems and a Song of Despair*
she points at the cheap threaded bracelet around my ankle
it says *poet*

I give it to her
she places one hand over her heart   rubs it

in her outstretched hand a thick lopsided tomato
she reaches in her pocket   hands me a blue shell

she makes a small curtsy   points at me   she smiles
her teeth bright onyx glitter in the afternoon sun.

LEMON VERBENA
for Pauline and Nadia in Berkeley

I fell asleep last night dreaming of zebra chickens scratching soil
in a garden of lemon verbena
gooseberries hummed their arrival into my room
their eyes bright parasols of sleep
onions in the yard already dug and served
I could linger brown in the shade of these orange trees
watch my heart outgrow its hurt
this body a nest a tree built out of wheat-colored straw
Pauline offers up her magic laugh to a handful of statice and queen
     anne's lace
we assemble under a tree for photos
our fingers plaited into sister braids
our yesterday worries scrawny lines between us.

MOONFLOWER
for (JP) Juliet Howard

who will remember our poems
their lives blue petal petunias
their lips scolding sky
who will remember these lines
scattered geography trailing moonflower
their pearl-white throats
ripping red at night

III

GLORY

GLORY

Most days before he was born
sun refused to leave her doorway

smells of nutmeg, Angostura bitters
and her own dust peppered the hallways

thyme, eucalyptus, lucky leaves   and small
reels of blond cobweb thread lined the bedside table

she had spent most of the nine months before his birth
sewing little white hats, sleeping gowns

booties, and blankets. It seems like that boy housed in her body
for ten months or more, and by the time he was born none of her

handmade fineries could fit him. Finally her water broke
streaking a patterned ribbon along the bathroom and hallway floors

it was a strange color, the midwife said,
a mix of pink pomerac and dark Chablis

oh God, spare him, she prayed as she waited
in the bamboo rocking chair that her grandfather had lacquered

color of dried rosemary leaves. From the second-floor balcony she
could see the family graveyard, elegant mansions of ochre & lime

she greeted Pa every morning with rose hips and brandy
sprinkled on the raw earth, and every night two white Oya candles

keep my boy well Pa, lord she had so many names
for that one child, Asah and Rufus, Marley and Anslem

he was born when Sunday slipped behind the moon
into the wide oval veranda of the midwife's arms

puce was the color of his skin
she called him Glory.

MAMA

A child at my house calls me mama
he's placed moon in my ear
who is that girl who births a son
to hip the world
to name him sweetness
finally I have become wise woman
an oasis of wild fish
cut and scored by my Arima red dirt hands.

FIRSTBORN
for Malik Izaak

Malik walks into my open arms
first visit home three months after kidney surgery

my heart beats against his puffy North Face vest
his face swollen he tilts his head down to the side

his chin a deepening cleft
more like his father's each year

I kiss his puffed cheeks
his steel-brown eyes

warrior that he is
he's never looked more beautiful

WHAT TO DO ON THE FIRST ANNIVERSARY OF YOUR SON'S DEATH

Write a poem to him
cry as much as you want
sleep as late as you want
stay in bed and dream about your son
look at his pictures
put his pajamas on
ask your lover to bring you coffee
drink your coffee black

do not look at Facebook
do not read his friend's posts
call your daughter-in-law
do not take calls from others
do not talk to the fools at the cemetery
do not take business calls
do send off your press release to at least
four colleges it will make you feel useful

build an altar of white tulips clear crystals
white candles   white sage
fill a wineglass with water
burn some sage
pray for peace
pray for courage
light two white candles
one for the year that's passed
one for the year to come

put on your cerulean-blue sweater
with your sea-green scarf
after all it is the color of mother nature's digestive tract
dot your earlobes and wrist with lavender oil

fuss over your lipstick
go to Pillow's for brunch
do not order wine
order the wild African bark strawberry tea

remember the time you introduced your son
to earl grey tea, then the next time you saw
him he introduced you to lady grey tea
when you exclaimed, *I didn't know they made lady grey tea*
and he said *yes, mummy, dey make it special fer you*
special just fer you girl
everybody laughed at the table, but you were serious

I was a teenager when Malik was born
Mom was disappointed and scared
yet she was hopeful
she told my husband and me she would help us with the baby
if we stayed in college

it was my grandmother's cackling
that brought the hens to the yard to be fed
it was the broken chips of roasted corn and
cracked barley that eventually brought the eggs
brown and regal in their own pile of straw

it was the mother's mournful wailing
that brought the moon to sit between
her knees   ah take two listen
she sound like she was between heaven and hell
rum and holy water

my face full ah worries
ah throw a memory in she purse
braid amaryllis and rosary beads in she hair
she like she black coffee and she Rémy

ah throw de ache in de first garbage can I see
misery eh ah color that does look good on me nah

TENTH-GRADE FLY
for Walt Taylor, Malik's dad

There's a new Tribe album all day there's celebration
then the death news after that I feared for my life
after that I feared for my country this red eye soggy and broken
life's a looking glass a little salt
that sampling of sea

Where in the Bible does it say we should not question God
days of swearing   not eating sleeping speaking
we walked the fields in search of you

Anybody if you see my son tell him I'm gone searching
with his dad   in the bag there's fish meat and bread
there's milk and the bones of small goats to wash and dry
into sharp arrows for the hunt

In one week all the leaves smell like your hair after Afro Sheen
you tenth-grade fly and slightly dangerous
your rhyme schemes got heat

Finally this morning river sings
sun is bright and we are smiling
now all we need are your eyes to guide
us into this aging.

Dear son,
Please come home soon.

HEIRLOOM CORN

Her arms a nest opening & closing   always opening closing growing a nest
for nurturing a nest for comfort   for years   we built homes for sparrows to
create living and beauty even in the midst of tremendous loss once my twin
entered the story of my body   my temple I was never alone I was always
paired up loved by my twin brother who Mama said she did not have a name
for she already had a boy a big mouth to feed and now she just wanted a girl
she told me when I was nineteen and pregnant
*if you want a baby girl only hang around your friends who have girl babies not
boys there are enough of them in the world*
but Mom I said I came with a boy that must mean something   we grew
stout and cherished seven months in our mother's warm room with every
half moon   my body tells me to be alert despite the ravages of loss be alert
be noble and proud to be a dream keeper   my body wants to be near any
space where it can hold seawater my twin brother
first one to touch my face first one to greet to kiss farewell arms a nest
last time I wore a baby on my hips I threw him there like a sack of heirloom
corn precious and growing he cooed screamed and held on catching the air
with his teeth
opening & closing.

FOR ALEM

I watch Alem dance
and run wild through the house

he is excited at my visit
he patiently explains why it is dark so early

because the sun is leaving
and the moon is coming in, he says

his heart shines brightly in his eyes

a two-year-old is educating me
we play together his soft curls caressing my face

who is this boy
sent to smile my heart

*I wanna go on the bus
let's go outside*, he says

his persistence reminding me of outings with
my adventure boy

let's go he says, I hide my tears
love his baby smell

I can't say *baby* anymore
he quickly reminds me he is a big boy now

he signs a drawing for Auntie Ceni
to wish her happy birthday

on the phone he says *I love you*
and shouts a parting, I wanna come to your house

his mouth lofty and veiled in summer glow, laughing wide
the way he will one day as he shouts his first roller coaster ride.

IV

SALUTE TO THE WOMEN WHO LIFTED ME

The only way forward is with a broken heart.
—Alice Walker

I started 2016 with a challenge in my heart and head. Having just lost my son, my body hurt all over, my vision seemed to be going, I feared I'd die. I knew that the universe was not yet done with me. In the weeks that followed, I cried, prayed, hid in my house, burned white sage, and read my favorite poems over and over. I went to readings just to listen and slowly began writing again. I formed an online writing circle, Elma's Heart Circle, in honor of my mother, who taught me to love poems. I asked other poets to write with me. Then I asked Cheryl Clarke to exchange Sunday poems with me. I felt lighter and partially whole again, safe again.

A WOMAN SPEAKS
for Audre Lorde on her eightieth birthday

I pick a bunch of hibiscus blooms
What lessons shall I learn from the spell of their senses?

For a long time I wanted to be a poet but was insecure about my writing
and often talked myself out of that dream. I was hard on myself. The thing I
loved as much as poems was flowers. I knew that there was something to be
learned by observing them.

On my nightstand that year,
I placed a bunch of red, peach, and white amaryllis blossoms,
some with their tongues already peering out,
others half open. I wanted to observe the delicate way they broke skin,
pushing ever so slightly into the vortex of the room . . .
petals unbruised, lighting the room like so much sun after a rainstorm.

I first met Audre Lorde at a gathering at Hunter College in New York City.
The event was held to name a student library in her honor. I was in love with
her poetry, but very scared and intimidated by her larger-than-life presence.
She was not only brilliant; she was brave, fierce, and absolutely stunning.
At some point in the evening she came over and introduced herself to me. I
told her that I was a novice poet. The truth is, by then I had been writing for
many years, but I was almost speechless in her presence.

We chatted a bit, and to my surprise she took an immediate interest and
invited me to take a women-of-color class she was offering that fall. I began
to stammer and told her that I was not a student at Hunter. She did not bat
an eye, instead saying, *That's no problem; I'm giving you a personal invitation.
I am looking forward to seeing you then?* She smiled and, in that alluring
Caribbean accent of hers, wished me a fine evening. My heart was beating
outside of my chest, I am sure.

During the weeks that followed, I decided that I was not going to accept her
invitation, because I was not a real poet.

Dear Audre,

Thank you for the invitation to take your class. I am thinking that with my young son, school, and work, I may not have enough time to travel into the city to take your class.

Three weeks later . . .

> Dear Audre,
>
> *I think that I may be experiencing a change of heart. Today I read poems from* The Black Unicorn. *It reminded me of how much I want to be a poet, a badass, grown woman poet like you.*

I am filled with birth stories and moon's sickled lamp

Now and then I sit quiet cup ah coffee in meh hand
listen hear de words hisssing
draw magic in dem breath
rest crimson in de damp gauze of girlhood

dem words weave faded straw into colorful baskets
they hang heart and lungs
teeth and bone
    meh head almost fall off de side ah meh face
        an fall fall on meh dauter womb

dem words loop poems 'round moon neck
   and if yuh hear dem heard em write dem down
we ah write ah write dem down

A wooden fist cracks cut and bruise she small black face de kitchen smell ah
  cod fish n
fresh baked bread he strike she cuss she
then sit to eat she bread
she eye de hammer de fry pan de sharp edge ah she mother table between
  them

      She pen waiting
pretending not to need.

I cannot say what was on the bed the day I left.

        —Aracelis Girmay

Dear Audre,

I wrote a new poem today. I cannot wait to read it in your class
tomorrow.

Morning cracked with sharpness
the girl whose hands I wear
will learn to fight   will learn to write
will learn to eat poems

I am the third generation of daughters whose mother worked as a domestic
pinching scrambling to provide food   It always comes back to food
        Immigrants are
always hungry
always tired
always working three jobs
trying to catch that dream

I am still thinking about the clay-pot coolness of my first lover's skin
her bister nipples how her bare chest rose and fell
the pillow wet with our woes

To class we brought our hips grapes lettuce sun our pens tablets and sharply
      oiled faces
how our fingertips swelled rolling rough against the ocean of words
it was the year for blue moon and long impressions of sweeping light
earth opened her mouth belched up her tethered roots
her curse her roar her wings her laughing body a kite rising

Audre's voice opening the door of day
I wanted her words to heal/hold me
I stepped her Candombe
lit the room with kora and white sage
poems fell like Florida water
a red restless in the shuffle of feet on the early afternoon floor

That fall I wore only dresses
lavender-jasmine perfume scarlet senorita lipstick deep space voodoo blush
low necklines dangling cowrie earrings and violet-blue rice paper journals

Is that not what it takes to be a poet?

On the first day I arrived at Audre Lorde's class without any poems. In my
anxiety to make class, I forgot my poems at work.

She called on me first to share a poem. With deep embarrassment, I told her
I had forgotten them. She asked me what kind of poet I was to come to class
without my work. She asked what kind of poet I wanted to be.
I did not know.

I was humiliated. I wanted to cry, but I never forgot my poems again, not
then, not now. Audre told our class Poetry Is Not a Luxury. She said we
should use words as weapons or not use them at all.

That night she asked, "What would happen if you wrote the things you really wanted to say? Who is holding a gun to your head and preventing you from saying the things you must say?"

In that moment I began to sob. I knew that I was the one "holding the gun" to my own head. There was weeping around the room. Then Audre asked, "So who's going to bring the tissues?"

That year I worked harder than I ever did before. At the end of class, Audre asked me to visit her in St. Croix. I did not go to St. Croix. I was too afraid.

Not going remains one of the biggest regrets of my life, but I learned a lot from that experience. Years later, one of Audre's friends told me that Audre really admired and loved my use of Trinidadian dialect in my work.

I wrote a poem for Audre and had a chance to read it to her at the I Am Your Sister international conference held in her honor. The poem is one of my old signature poems titled "A Dyke in a Dress." It was one of the last times I saw her. I am so thankful for the lessons I learned from her and am still trying to be the hardworking, truthful poet she saw in me so many years ago.

1962, EVERYBODY PRETTY

all de neighbor chiren ha good hair
dougla girls with ribbons braided in their locks

everybody pretty
except me

all de girls have nice long curls
except me with de few
notty dry peas for bangs on top

press it, daddy say
ah good hot comb go do, gramma say

ah perm go last longer, tanty say
what stupidness leave she hair alone, that's mummy talking

everybody body pretty
not me

someday you will learn to live wid your beauty
and your talent chile

not everybody know to write dauter
bless yuh little hand that choose de pen

may the rain gods water your tears
and wash you of shame darling

may sunset find you
maturing confident in your loveliness.

FOR THE LOVE OF TENNYSON & LANGSTON

Bless my mother and her slingshot of poems
bless her kiss and her tears
as we prayed every night beside our little bed

bless my mother her red mist of words
bless my mother's hands her unmarried ring finger
bless her scraps of favorite poems hidden in cupboards

bless her haikus and vowels
her light melodious noise filling our house
bless her narratives and her odes

bless her Lord Tennyson
and the poem she recited until the day she died
bless her favorite poem

her "Charge of the Light Brigade"
and her Battle of Balaclava, 1854
bless her pride at finding Langston Hughes

at fifty bless her excitement at college graduation
bless her flip phone
and her nurse's cap
her stiffly starched white uniform

bless my mother and the way she never spoke bad of my father
lord knows she really had so much to tell
bless her big hugs and her narrow kind eyes

bless her wide green skirt and
her delicate feet made for dancing
bless her beautiful garnet lips and her bell of a voice

her hands making straw hats
bless her whispering and her laughter
bless her laying on of poems

bless her fixing of shattered dreams
bless my mother and her braid around her head
bless her lean copper frame and the twins it bore

bless her steady breath to my cheek
bless her neck and its long banjo song
her voice piecing wounds into poems

bless my beautiful mother and the seven dollars
she left pinned to that note
dear Cherry, please take a cab to church
Jesus loves you so does Mommy.

*I found that note three years after she died. What joy.

ON MCKINLEY DRIVE
birthday poem for Mom

There is a small house at the edge of McKinley Drive
where the road turns dirt and the river runs clear
there is an off-white porch that leaks
in rainy season
there where the floorboard dips and the door creaks
there where my navel string bury and meh twin brother
heart grow fruit
there where you braided my hair and added satin bows
in that house, that beautiful house that held my mother's songs, her poems
        and the names she called her children
Russell, Cheryl.
It was Cheryl-Allison when I did something bad
And it was Girlie when I did things right
In that small house we dressed for church and knelt around
our small bed praying for the sick and shut-in for loved ones and God's
        mercy to see us through that day
and every morning her lovely voice would fill the house
as she fixed breakfast folded clothes or swept floors
the door of her arms flung open
to squeeze, to comfort, to hold
that good love, a star called Mommy.

On the road from Amsterdam to Stresa, the Italian fishing port where
Hemingway once stayed, my mother and I oooohed, moaned, and waved at
the fields of sunflowers growing lush and thick. They seemed to wave back,
bowing and racing the white light that hugged the bust of windows speeding
to gorgeous Lake Maggiore on the edge of the Italian coast. Someone said
they grew them in abundance to make sunflower oil. We were in awe of their
toothy grins and must have passed two million of them, each more beautiful
than the next, each more exotic and tempting than the other. I tried to count
them, all lined up like soldiers in their yellow helmets. In that parade we
passed so many viewings, tales for weddings, conceptions, christenings, and
funerals, their dark heads blush and ready for birth. We were broken up that
year, love, still my mouth watered for your breast.
You my sun goddess with stem erect and brown reminding me of your long
proud neck gleaming with sweat after each evening's romp.

CHANGE PURSE FILLED WITH FOREIGN COINS
for Mom

On the coffee-stained bureau
onyx earrings black as piano keys
early morning snuck in through the wooden
plantation shades each measuring the light
a blue wind troubled the cotton curtains
her light breathing went easily unnoticed
an only daughter I had reconciled early in life
I would be the one to take care of her
I was happy she had been a good mother
she wore high heels almost to the end
her change purse filled with foreign coins
her white cotton panties
her little wig drying on the bathroom rod
lovable
time runs out
age defies all
been one long joyous road.

YOU BRAID YOUR HAIR

the day after your mother's passing
you wash her clothes
shop for her burial outfit
a peach linen blazer
white lace blouse
white tea-length prairie skirt

social security freezes your joint account
next day her renewed driver's license comes in the mail
you take the LIRR to deliver her clothing
fall to pieces when the conductor says *St. Albans*
that was always your meeting place
she always picked you up there

you've lost her insurance policy
New York Life refuses to release her burial check
for thirty-eight years she paid down that damn bill
that's most of your son's life
when you finally find it they still won't cut a check
say they must notify the beneficiary first

you give away your mother's table, chairs, bed
you sign the thank-you cards
you can't mail them
after all they're not wedding invitations

you say *thanks so much* you cry a lot
wear your mother's sunglasses and sweater
use her old glasses at poetry readings

months later you unbraid your hair pack a weekend bag
life wears your drunk cave like a tin crown
hollow and pretty   you fill the corners
of each room with bitter bright marigolds
Mexican flowers for your dead.

THE HOME YOU LEFT LONG AGO
poem for Aracelis Girmay

There is a moment
when you don't even realize you are hungry
then a poet stands before you
a poet exquisite her mouth a topaz city
filled with hummingbirds, blue herons, and marigolds

you listen to her hum
she's an orchestra
her body the home you left so many years ago
she speaks her words serenading you
and that platter of tenderness is placed before you
you dig in with both hands
her words lilt bamboo stalks propping up your aching heart

you take in every sob every breath
every flame every god
    she's pregnant says she is out of breath
in that way a healing makes you out of breath

I am saying she is
sermon baptism scripture
her poem a kiss rooted deep along the spine
her violet-blue mouth scooped out of a trini calabash
held up by brown hands

she has your mother's voice
your mother's unbruised hands
until one day she ends up
washing white folks' drawers for she green card

your mother's hands scrubbing cleaning
bringing you soup
wiping away your tears

your mother making herself invisible to stay alive
your mother taking care of other people's daughters
to feed you to hold a warm compress against your forehead
every other weekend

your mother reassuring you
we will be together again
soon I love you daughter

for a moment you hate her
her voice calls your words from its hiding place
her poem calls and calls you
like every ocean you have ever known.

A CENTO FOR WINNIE MANDELA

Sister, teach me how to paint my lips silent
in the face of these atrocities

your body an empty plate
living in the shade

of your husband's slow left hand
your once bright eyes

coffee-colored stone
and the loud crashing of glass

in that bed of joy and affliction
the brown spill of bodies

a slow procession of military predators
standing guard

teach me, sister, to pray your name
to embalm my eyes with your ghost

NTOZAKE'S CRIMSON ORCHIDS

Night was discarding her soft shell
rain swept day without apology

walking barefoot across hot asphalt
her parched body a serpent

she dared me to follow
there is no light as mistrustful as high noon

I woke to find her gone
my body holds seawater

blue-breasted robins
green seaglass

mother-of-pearl shells
when I pray

there is no light as mistrustful as high noon
even the moon is telling lies

there is a garden where the salsa dancers gather
Zaki's hair an unruly cluster of trees

you will find her there
weaving crimson orchids in her hair.

RODLYN'S ROOTS
after Rodlyn H. Douglas

her laughter shook the ground on which we stood
a red basket filled with bee balm chocolate mint
heirloom tomatoes slung over her arm

eye makeup bright as monarch butterflies
open prairie shirt with toenails to match
always the poet-preacher she schooled me

here is cinnamon oil from Sri Lanka
rub it on to chase away mosquitoes
yellow dock root for indigestion

flaxseed for constipation
senna or turkey rhubarb if you find
you still can't go

Chinese motherwort angelica root
and cinnamon bark for menstrual cramps
a hot water bottle will fix that too

tell Patricia anise for milk secretion
when she nursing baby Ellis
white sage to clear the air for good dreams

horny goat weed will increase sperm
cayenne and ginseng
if yuh want to keep de fire in yuh bed

next minute she was gone
then I spotted her red specs peering into some woman's
purple sage
her laughter breaking ground where they stood

END OF LENT
kimo for Rodlyn H. Douglas

Big pan ah fry fish in she basket   thyme
oregano chives scallions
spiced jersey beets   we eat

HOWL FOR MAYA ANGELOU

After you left, Maya
I tried not to scare the wind with my howling
and when the Hudson River refused my tears
I forgot the sound of your voice
then I recited the names of morning glories
lilacs blue petunias & Maya's mint
after passing a field of purple
I followed the hurricane path through the Middle Passage
that gave birth to your slingshot songs

MAYA CALLING JUNE JORDAN
a zuihitsu

On my writing table
two diamond wedding bands
seven tangerine mini carnations

pink magic marker
Nicole Sealey's *Ordinary Beast*

I hate Ceni today she's at Coney Island
our favorite beach with friends
I'm at the writing table
on it three purple pens a cat journal

cobalt-blue nail polish
extra-strength Tylenol
Apidra insulin pen

clove oils turmeric the ghost of Frida Kahlo

1988—Kissing Martine was such sorrow

dat woman hang a
do not disturb sign outside she window

in the dream Maya Angelou calls June Jordan
to she yard *Acakee Ackee Mama*

I never get good sleep anymore

brother takes my green arm
it's time to walk in sunshine   he says
time to climb tamarind trees
time to swing from branch to fruit-laden branch
brush your hair with coconut furs
he says

girl, eat bowls of callaloo
then follow carefully
the footsteps of your words
written in lines of exalted hues.

ADRIENNE
for Adrienne Rich

Tonight Lucille and Audre
hold hands

while waiting for Adrienne to come
just girlfriends arranging flowers

peonies   hydrangeas   baby's breath
Boston fern

summer quilts in the sun
pink lemonade swilled with fresh fruit

just girlfriends talking
about the glow of moon rock and the color of soil

it's possible we could go dancing
says Lucille, in her playful way

I propose some time for writing
says Audre, in her proper Cariacou twang

maybe there will be time for both after listening to new poems, says Lucille

tonight bedsheets will smell of sage
the kitchen of oxtail stew and coconut rice

come sister put your ear to my heart
hear the coming roar of that river called Adrienne

SAY HER NAME: BREONNA TAYLOR
for Breonna Taylor killed by police in her home

That last summer in Liberty we made paper boats
sat our troubles and sailed them in the lake
we laughed like schoolgirls
our dream a fingertip's distance away
we did not know our world would get so ugly

we did not know hundreds of Black mothers doing day's work killing themselves
did not know sisters getting raped in the name of marriage
we did not know sixteen-year-old Gynnya McMillen
who died alone in a juvenile detention center in Kentucky
because she refused to remove her sweatshirt

we did not know Mya Hall a black trans woman killed
alleged to be driving a stolen car
did not know Meagan Hockaday mother of three girls
killed in her home by police responding to a domestic issue
did not know Breonna Taylor killed by police in her home

we did not know Sandra Bland
Rekia Boyd
Kisha Michael
Tanisha Anderson

Shantel Davis
Miriam Carey
Eleanor Bumpurs
did not know   did not know   did not know

we did not know
even the Catskill Mountains
with her wide embrace could not save us
we did not know to take a selfie of each other's ache

Black woman your heart is everything I believe in
your breath is enough
to save this trembling earth

may sun wrap you in her glitter gold sari
may the wind drape your head in bright orange heliconias
may we never cease to call your name
                        call your name
                              call your name

Here's an apology for your legendary life.

V
LET'S MAKE A DRUM

BRAVE
for Ceni

Our bed grows lions and weeping willow trees
two crow's nests with hatching frizzle fowls inside
Shelly the cat gives me the side eye
she can never find her food dish
it's overrun by potted plants

again this week we are out of Fancy Feast
our socks mismatched
most of them have run away from home
the fridge is sparse 'cept for garlic knots
and fried rice

so many smart books on the shelf
begging to be read
now they cuss and look away from
the African village of fertility dolls poking out
their dusty chests

our sofa grows quilts and bamboo pillows
a fancy bird glass from Ikea
this morning I fell over the broom
with the ninety-cent dustpan attached
damn no Tiger Balm   one more pain patch on the shelf
we need to toss a coin for that

the kettle hissing on the stove
one hardboiled egg for breakfast
a fancy crystal tray filled with dust and address labels
let's just be brave and throw it all away.

CALL HER DELPHINIUM

The day after our worst fight
she brought me a huge bouquet of mixed flowers
cosmos dusty millers delphiniums wax
hydrangeas with petals torn
bruised like our hearts

she clipped the stems evenly
added warm water to the pitcher
and all the sugar one can find in the house of two diabetic lovers   still
wax spilled her needles on the kitchen counter
floor glass tabletop

a single iris hung comatose
she held the bulb like she wanted to sew its purple heart back
almost with the care she would use to sew us back together
she stared at me
I looked away

and thought—
dot her eyes with asters
braid her body into two leis of blue delphiniums
my lips bitter stained marigolds at the garden of her thighs
the neon skeleton of my teeth calling her filthy names.

REVOLUTION

Take no love because of lonely
learn the body's kiln
its ravines & curves
steam moan by your own hands
skirt the embroidery of death
call your ancestors to witness
glow   feed on your own hands
to weep with joy
that too is a revolution.

BELOVED COUNTRY
for Ceni

Twenty years later
I watch her sleep
pillow as gown

did I see her face or mine
two uneven amulets
nipples like the face of God

did her hands or mine trace tips of thighs down
down to that beloved country
where the righteous dance
wide against this ample day?

I PREFER

                              I prefer

a stranger's quick tongue
to a familiar soggy mouth
I prefer wind in trees to the
hacking cough of love songs
prefer the harsh slap of tart strawberries
to a pillow wet with woes

                              I prefer

burnt orange to cardinal red
prefer passion fruit to granny smith apples
I prefer to write about moon
than poems that rhyme
I prefer a banjo
to the white skulls of piano keys

                              I prefer

to be desired by stars
than by the first long day of summer
I prefer to sell my heartbreak to the world
than to harvest unrequited love
I prefer deep-space voodoo blush
to well-aged Bordeaux wine

                              I prefer

to wear a bindi on my forehead
cowbell rings in my nose
I prefer to share my lover
than to have her grow moldy in my bed
I prefer to wear a borrowed wedding dress
and drink my salsa harsh and rowdy

                    I prefer
to lament the past
than ask permission of my future
I prefer never to look back
my limbs adorned with christmas ornaments
I prefer my saffron mouth worn bright
in memory of you.

                                        after Rodlyn

ON REPEAT
A kimo

Oh aw, babe please stop, she says, every
time I take her back with my red
brush *Do that again. Please.*

PRAISE FOR HER NOISY LAUGHTER

Praise kiss of cherry blossoms blanketing the land
praise the poet's voice loud enuf
to still gunshots
praise our words exchanged for currency of cowrie shells
praise rain shaking rows of trees
praise the Sunday brunch lazing into dinner
praise the red and peach peppers
cubes of sun-glazed yellow squash
praise her hands washing parsley leaves
and the cornish hens sliced thin
praise her noisy laughter a rainstorm cracking sky
praise the cumin, crushed ginger, pink Himalayan salt
praise our smoky kitchen of ten thousand spices
praise her teeth nuzzling my neck
and the tart taste of lemon-lime running down my chest
praise her hips that be oil drum then steelpan trampoline
praise night and her brown thighs
her sex a glistening sari
voice a cracked tiara wailing in a wounded city

HOW TO MAKE ART

her sharp mouth a bright silver revolver
fingers a scorched iron train
stop
      that hurts
sweeter than I found you
next day
          open each section girl
girl you make me weep
        is sun leaving
I always want to praise sky & Ceni
      my night rider
twenty-two years and I can still drown in her wildness
all the while praying calling Jesus   Jesus
who gets to be called daddy first
         to paint your toes bright orchid
teeth disguised as new bones
      to tame a wild woman   worship her like a poem.

TRADE
in the time of a pandemic

To keep safe I cut a swatch of African fabric from the dress
I'm wearing to make a hand-sewn mask

once at a marketplace in Gambia
I traded a handful of cigarettes for this beautiful dress

on the fabric long-legged hyenas and hamerkops
in colors of dark red sail across God's pristine land

bless the giggles of mothers and young girls in the marketplace
as they trade their hand-painted cloth for American jeans and lip gloss

bless the candle and starch
bless the hands that forged that cotton into a thing of beauty

bless the high-life dance
the two a.m. dark the coffee bitter black

SATURN RETURNING

The night before Grandma Ada died
she asked if I had a mirror what would I see looking back
my dad's head tucked in the pocket of my arms
we'd go to sleep dreaming of ocean and my twin brother
riding Grandpa Rufus's brown donkey Mo
on his way back home to meet us

Once we awoke my parents would be feasting on their marriage
this time they'd be cooking a fat calf for both sides of the family
my father would not be drunk then
he'd be holding my mother by her delicate waist
they would do the two-step
It must be glorious to wake up with married parents
and know the joy they are harvesting is you and your twin brother

If I ever saw moon meandering across my night
I would tell her to bring my twin home
because his black exquisite bark of skin
because his eyes generations come and gone
because his hands a healing sage
because his feet forever crossing Middle Passage
landing on the delta delivering free humans
because the full bush of curls on his head

This time I'd give my left arm to wrap
throw it around him and never let go
I'd place his needs ahead of my longing
moon in Saturn returning
sugary breath of Jesus on her lips
old red wood fan swirling lazy round and round.

I AM NOTHING COMPARED TO
911 pantoum—after Milton Kessler

the pleading eyes against the airplane window
the tumbling frame of father bookkeeper son
the reporter's livid lens
day eleven of the ninth month

the tumbling frame of father bookkeeper son
the long red tresses flaming into shoulder blades
the reporter's livid lens
September two thousand one

the long red tresses flaming into shoulder blades
the black charred Manolo Blahniks
I am nothing compared to September two thousand one
Dali's frozen clock

the black charred Manolo Blahniks
Atta's crumbled mind
Dali's frozen clock
the treble of God's ear

Atta's crumbled mind
Rwanda
the treble of God's ear
I am nothing compared to the Middle Passage

Rwanda
Goree Island's slave depot
I am nothing compared to the Middle Passage
the jumpers at Two World Trade Center

Goree Island's slave depot
Treblinka
the jumpers at Two World Trade Center
the half-melted copper bracelet

Treblinka
the tumbling frame of father bookkeeper son
the half-melted copper bracelet
day eleven of the ninth month

HERE: IN OUR TIME OF WAR

Here are my fingers
Use them as fire starters

Here are my hands
use them to write this world into peace

Here are my shoulder blades
use them as drum to summon ancestors

Here are my words
use them as provocation as resistance

Here are my eyes
tears on the windowsill

Wiping them quick
so no one sees

How I miss my child
how I miss him

Here is Charlie Wilson's CD
the last gift Malik gave me

Use it as clarity
use it as affirmation

that you're blessed   that I'm blessed

Here is my propped-up heart
use it as a sweet spot for nesting

Here are my poems
use as dirge for dancing
use as collateral for taking back our planet

Here is my arthritic spine
recycle and use it
use it to plant trees

DREAMSCAPE

These are rough times
to dance close, to whisper
in the crook of your arms
to glitter with night

a throat damaged with grief
to know each swell intimately
saw life way up ahead
ran to grab its dust
sweet william braided in my crown

last time I wore my baby on my hips
I threw him there like a sack of grits

love bless my stomach
all the seawater it has held
all the insulin needles it has caressed

you speak and laugh with your eyes did you know that
my body my body was never alone it danced naked in the yard

then a rainstorm called me bitter my heart said beautiful woman   testing
        blood sugar
after whisky shots   pork browning
in good New Zealand butter

I wear my Vera Wang wedding gown to Easter dinner
to sit alone dine on sweet wine and cornmeal polenta

if this is the end
I'll wear my rose quartz necklace
enter when Aretha Franklin calls
sisters are doing it   doing it for themselves

LET'S MAKE A DRUM: LET THERE BE SINGING

I walk into the new apartment
throw white wine in corners for my dead
a panorama of light pulls me to the windows tall and bright this warms me
yes yes finally I found my place this mad city has worn me down I run so fast
I become tree stump when I awoke from sleep my hair was straw my poem
was the small child killed last week
I flew became purple martin ate mosquitoes and small fish

In our month of words we shared and shed fear skin rage sex flamed like
        bonfire
I don't want to have regrets but how I wish I was still that girl pulling petals
        to make bouquets feathers to make hats voices to make choirs
let's not exoticize poverty or privilege it ain't need no savior
in fact girl your glass ceiling hangs as low as fucking mine let's make a family
        family
family   cook love   love
            love soup corn straw and poems

get me beet soup a chorus of birds
and a white Obeah shawl while we wait for beauty
let's make a book a palace to dance in
fruit to feed our young
let's make a continent a kite let's make a drum
a knife a hymn a torch a chant
Ibeji waist beads Ndebele neck rings let's be tribal let's cook and seduce
let there be singing and sweet melons for summer let's make America better
than we found it let's dig up our Bantu drums steelpans koras our ancestral
voices stronger than they left it
holla let our words read palms throw cowrie shells predict futures with tarot
        cards
let's pray and make babies daughters let's make blood who knows better than
        us how to do that